TOP 20 REASONS WHY STARTUPS FAIL

By Karo Olori
Copyright© Karo Olori 2019

A comprehensive guide highlighting the main reasons that can cause a business venture to fail, how these failures can be avoided and overcome.

Disclaimer

This e-book has been written for information purposes only. Every effort has been made to make this eBook as complete and accurate as possible. However, there may be mistakes in typography or content. Also, this e-book provides information only up to the publishing date. Therefore, this eBook should be used as a guide-not as the ultimate resource.

The purpose of this eBook is to educate. The author and the publisher don't warrant that the information contained in this eBook is fully complete and shall have neither liability not responsibility to any person or entity with respect to any loss or damage caused or alleged to be caused directly or indirectly by this eBook.

Preface

Success and failure are equally unpredictable and unavoidable in every new business venture. In spite of similar odds, some startups succeed while others are doomed for failure. The book- the top 20 reasons that can lead to startup failure and how following in the steps of successfully launched businesses you can learn to avoid them, will be a good guide. So, in case you are thinking of wearing your entrepreneurial hat, this book can prove to be a good read on the key factors that can transform your business and help you steer clear of failure.

Contents

Preface 3
Introduction 4
Top 20 Reasons Why Some Startups Fail 5
   1. Market Related Problems 5
   2. Financial Problems 6
   3. Wrong Business Model 6
   4. Weak Team Structure 7
   5. Wrong Product Fitment 7
   7. Lack of Marketing 8
   8. Poor Customer Support 9
   9. Poor Communication 10
   10. Fizzled out Passion 10
   11. Legal Issues 11
   12. Lack of Cash Flow 11
   13. Unable to Generate Financing 12
   14. Unable to Expand/Grow 12
   15. Poor Networking 13
   16. Wrong Timing 13
   17. Late Entrant 14
   18. Discord Among Partners 14
   19. Fraud 15
   20. Lack of Innovation 15
How To Avoid and Overcome the Failure of Your Startup 17
   ✓ Failure Can Be Positive 17
   ✓ Consistent and Constant 17
   ✓ Solutionize! 18
   ✓ Begin Small and Scale Up 18
   ✓ Financial Management 19
   ✓ Envision 19
   ✓ Analyze 19

Introduction

When we talk about startups, we form a mental picture of the dotcom companies that sprang up in the 1990s. While it may have been made popular then, the term startup has a much older connotation. In reality, any business venture that is in its very 1st phase of operations is categorized as a startup. It can be a new Technology venture or something as small as a retail business run from the comforts of your very home. However, big or small, whatever the scale may be, every new venture is bound to face a set of challenges that can shake its foundations and cause it to come tumbling down. Irrespective of the size or nature of the business, risk is the one thing that is common across all new ventures.

The onset of risk is beyond the control of even the most seasoned entrepreneurs. This holds true if you are starting something new in your personal space as well. In spite of this unpredictability, there are some businesses that will not just survive but thrive in all their glory while others never see the light of the day. This is primarily because startups face certain challenges in their initial few years which are beyond their immediate control, and they are more vulnerable to environmental factors like market discords than established companies.

This book explores the top 20 reasons that contribute towards the failure of startups. It further seeks to analyze how startups that begin with promise end up as failures. Entrepreneurs will learn how new ventures can overcome and avoid such situations that threaten their success and existence. The book also juxtaposes startups that failed against the startups that succeeded in order to compile a comprehensive guide towards the road to success. And lastly, provide pointers towards launching and running a successful business venture in which, you can steer clear of failure.

Top 20 Reasons Why Some Startups Fail

Problems don't sneak in as individual spies; they attack as battalions. And, startups seem to be under constant attack from various unforeseen obstacles. Whether it is financial, legal, resource related or concerning the very product offering itself; the problems can seem never ending and can potentially prove to be fatal if not addressed at the right time. The list below contains the top 20 problems that new ventures face and how they can become reasons for their failure.

1. Market Related Problems

The market is volatile and changes constantly making it an extremely challenging environment for startups as well as established firms. While short term stock corrections may not impact startups, a substantial and sustained correction in the market can have a negative impact on startups. Every market downturn is different and has its own unique effects. Deep and long-lasting downturns like the one that happened in 2008-2010 are more likely to affect startups. Basically, if the market is down it severely affects your business valuations. Also, there will be less money being pumped into startups through venture capitalists as everyone tends to play safe when the markets are down.

On the other hand, a severe downturn in the market can also prove to be a blessing in disguise for startups in the long run even though it can make the situation tough in the short term. Employee retrenchment can push brilliant people to take risks and join startups. There is also the possibility of lesser competition provided you have funding as many others may not and they may be forced to fold-up. In short, if you can run a start-up successfully during a downturn, it is likely to become an industry leader in the long term.

Companies like Microsoft, Revlon, and FedEx were all exposed to an economic crash during their initial years of experience and they went on to become leaders in their respective industries. FedEx was conceptualized in the year 1965 and turned profitable only in the year 1973 and within the next 10 years it became the 1st US startup to reach $1 billion in revenues.

2. Financial Problems

The inception of creative thought in your mind is not enough to launch a start-up business. Finance plays an immensely important role in its success, especially in the initial few years of the business's existence. In order to maintain financial stability throughout its lifetime, it is important for the business to have enough cash flow to help it expand. But before that, it is essential to secure enough seed funding to launch your product as you have envisioned. Venturing out without taking finance advice can lead to a half-baked effort that usually ends in a failed launch. The latest example of financial failure is the Hongkong based LeSports. The sports streaming venture was forced out of business in early 2018 as it was unable to pay the much overdue rent. Although, finance was not its core issue as the company was plagued by many other problems, it failed to generate enough liquidity to manage expenses.

3. Wrong Business Model

You can't avoid failures or risks that come with a new business model. However, if you can effectively manage them, they can remain small and inexpensive. For this, you have to make sure that your business model is correct and relevant. It should be aimed at performing a job or solving a problem. If it is not helping the target customer in any manner, then the entire business becomes irrelevant and is doomed for failure.

A business model is severely flawed if it is generating more costs than revenues. An inability to establish proper delivery and procurement channels can be the direct result of an incorrect business model. No amount of brilliance in your value proposition can rescue your startup in such a case. The business model needs to work for the company as much as it does so for the product and its owner.

Take the example of Kingfisher airlines. India's full service private sector airline carrier was definitely a more expensive affair to fly. However, this did not cause its premature demise. The airline failed because of the business model on which it was working. After the acquisition of Air Deccan, the company started operating on very thin margins, a wrong business model that it could not sustain for long.

4. Weak Team Structure

Poor organizational or team structure cannot just impact your new venture financially but can also prove to be a strong deterrent towards maximizing sales for your product offering. A wrong selection of people in management positions is one of the major reasons why many startups fail to succeed. If the top management isn't made up of people who share a collective vision and are capable of guiding the fledgling organization towards growth, the business is bound to fail.

In spite of all the technological advancement, human beings are still an integral part of running any business even if it is an online venture. Having a weak team structure can also affect how your customers and employees get treated. In other words, it can have a severe impact on both internal as well as external functioning of the company. This point can be cemented further with the example of Pan American Airways. It is impossible to look at the history of commercial aviation and not see the name of this American giant. Costly, over paid acquisitions and excruciatingly slow decision making of the top management eventually led to its demise.

5. Wrong Product Fitment

'Product Market Fit' is an important concept that can define the success or failure of any new business. So, what is the meaning of this term? Simply put, it means launching your product in a market where it can satisfy that market. The product should be capable of fulfilling a gap or a demand or create one if required. For instance, if you are running a social networking business like Facebook then your market is defined as everyday members who require a constant social presence. This segment becomes your strongest market, and this is where your product should fit. However, if your product does not satisfy the targeted segment in which it is launched, then it is bound to fail. Additionally, a misfit, or a miscalculated launch, can negatively impact the product take-off and lead to its untimely demise. Take Stayzilla for example, the Indian homestay network startup had to fold its operations in just 12 years of its existence. In spite of receiving multiple rounds of funding, the company failed to generate enough interest in the Indian travel market. This was because, there was neither an extent of homestays nor dwellers when the company was launched. A classic example of wrong product fitment.

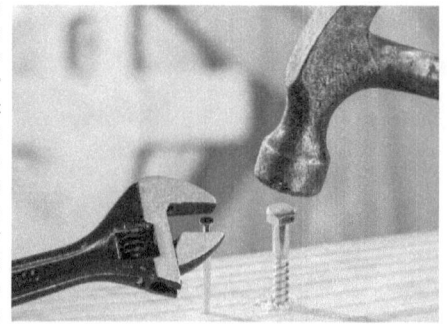

6. Competition

Imagine a scenario where a couple of weeks before you are set to launch a new product in the market, your competitor beats you to it. It spells out nothing but disaster for your new organization. As a startup, you don't have enough funds to divert a major chunk towards finding out what your competitor is up to. However, ignoring them entirely is also not the best way to proceed further. Technology today is capable of driving change at a pace that was non-existent a decade before. Know who your direct competitor is and be aware of the direction in which they are headed. Don't overdo it, though.

Let's take the classic example of Airbnb. While hotels were direct competition for it, the company did not start with an aim to take their market share. Airbnb founders focused on creating a unique product offering that could be accessed online and gave an indirect competition to the existing hotel/motel model. On the other hand, the recent demise of Jawbone can be attributed to competition killing its products off. In 2011 AliphCom, a Bluetooth speaker and headsets manufacturer changed its name to Jawbone and entered the mushrooming fitness wrist bands domain. After years of getting beaten up by Samsung and Fitbit, the new venture eventually called it quits and the company was liquidated in 2017. Even with enough funding, the company had to fold its operations as its products failed in comparison to the competition. Most experts feel that Jawbone also died as a result of over reaction to its competitors.

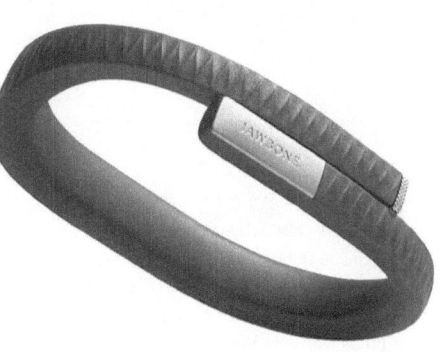

7. Lack of Marketing

Marketing usually takes a back seat in most companies without vision. This holds true for both startups, as well as well-established organizations. Seen as a supplementary department, marketing runs the risk of reduced funding when in fact, it is the most important department in the initial few years of operations for any startup. Any business in its early stages should understand the importance of sound marketing. A lack of an effective marketing strategy can fail to launch your product as you have envisioned. A business that refuses to acknowledge the importance of marketing is sowing seeds of its own disaster.

Let us conduct a brief comparison between Regus and WeWork to understand this concept better. Regus enjoyed over 21 years of monopoly in providing affordable office space solutions before it was challenged by WeWork. After just 9 years WeWork is worth about $47 billion whereas Regus is still at $3 billion. Regus's poor marketing as against the stellar effort put in by WeWork in the same department is one of the major reasons for the former's failure at success. In spite of having a two decade long head start, Regus failed to popularize its brand and generate a loyal client base. This also allowed a very late entrant to capitalize on the pioneer's shortcomings and build a stronger brand.

8. Poor Customer Support

No business can boast of a hundred percent satisfaction rate when referring to its customers. The customer today has become more tech- savvy and your poor customer service can find its way onto the social media before you have the time to react to it.

The customer service and support determine if your clients will remain loyal to you and help your business grow or not. As it is your one true chance to connect with the end-users, don't take it lightly. Since, a start-up is a new entrant, it takes the user some time to build trust. Offering poor customer service can spell disaster for the business before it even gets a chance to showcase its entire potential.

9. Poor Communication

A sub-standard, organizational communication can hurt your infant business. Communication is essentially the oil that is required for the smooth functioning of any business or organization. A communication gap is more likely to occur in a startup as rules are more flexible and usually, individual departments enjoy defining their own method of communication. While this may increase productivity initially, it cannot be considered as a sustainable model in the long run.

Even the minutest glitch in the communication machinery can have a long term impact on the effectiveness of the product in the market. This can eventually doom your business to failure. So, it is important to ensure that the wheels are always in motion. For this, the guidance has to percolate from the top management. Make sure that the standard of effective communication is maintained and modified with the changing market requirements. Don't let your startup come to a standstill.

10. Fizzled out Passion

You and your partner are busily burning the midnight oil wishing there were more hours in the day so you could dedicate them as well towards working on your startup. Once the business is launched you spend every waking moment planning for its success and expansion. As time passes, you or your partner may lose that edge that you once had. Your passion starts dwindling and you are no longer capable of investing the time required towards the new venture. It is a common scenario with numerous business ventures and the gradual fizzling out of passion and commitment leads to partners folding up shop. There can be a number of reasons for this. Perhaps you launched in a market that was highly saturated; you are not cut out for business; your passion lies elsewhere. According to Richard Branson, founder of the Virgin Group, generating profit should not be the whole and sole purpose behind launching a business. He feels that even if you have an excellent idea, it may not take off as planned if you are implementing it in a sector that you are not passionate about.

11. Legal Issues

Like marketing, the legal department also receives a step-son-like treatment by many startups. Businesses that fail to engage effective legal counsel before they start their venture open themselves to numerous risks that can prove to be fatal for their startup before it has even begun operations. By not hiring a legal service, you can open yourselves to the risk of not having proper, or the required licenses. Your organization can get registered under an incorrect legal structure having tax implications that can eat into your precious funding. At the very least, you are likely to end up with some form of improper documentation or another. Lack of legal protection can also expose you to copyright infringement or employee troubles.

12. Lack of Cash Flow

When you run a business, the cash flows both ways – into and out of the business. It is the responsibility of the business owner to ensure that there is a healthy flow in both categories. If your outflow is greater than your inflow, then you need to relook at certain aspects of your product and business model. Lack of cash in your business can mean that you will accumulate debt on the essentials you are required to procure for your product development and delivery. It is important to make sure that your business has enough positive cash flow as the market is volatile and you can be hit with a recession when your liquidity will be severely impacted.

Let us consider the example of Laundroid. It was developed by the Japanese company, Seven Dreamers and had the potential to transform the domestic landscape. The all in one product was designed to function as a washer, dryer, ironing, and folding robot machine. However, in the April of 2019, it was forced to fold its business venture before the product could even hit the stores. The company lacked cashflow and had accumulated immense debt. It owed nearly 2.25 billion Yen to over 200 creditors. Money can never be undermined in a startup situation.

13. Unable to Generate Financing

Everyone knows that setting up a business requires financing. While nearly all businesses start small, constant growth and expansion are the only ways in which they can continue to exist. In a startup, it is the responsibility of the founder to generate financing and make sure that there is enough cash flow in the business to meet the growing requirements. If you are unable to perform this part, then your company can fail through stagnation and lack of innovation. Karhoo, a cab aggregator and a company with its own price comparison tool and innovative concepts failed to remain in business and had to fold operations after just 2 years of its inception. They, reportedly, ended up blowing through a funding of nearly $250 million. The poor management and ineffective product failed to generate the required funding for sustenance and expansion.

14. Unable to Expand/Grow

It is common for startups to become stagnant even with enough financing. This is because growth and expansion are dependent on various other factors that may or may not be in your control. You can obtain finance but may have a flawed vision of the direction in which you want to expand your product line proving the entire experience to be a failure. Or, you are unable to capture the market as you had envisioned, and your competitors have already taken over leaving limited avenues for your growth.

Carrefour, the French hypermarket giant, was forced to fold operations in Singapore after 15 years. An organization that had once served as a pioneer introducing the very concept of hypermarkets in this beautiful city-state, failed to scale up and expand its operations beyond a few stores. While this was largely due to the competition from home grown stores, the real reason for this retreat is that the retail giant did not focus on expansion.

15. Poor Networking

A startup that has a pocket full of meaningful relationships can surely succeed. Networking has always been an important component of launching a new product or service. Your network also acts as a safety net and allows you to take risks while entering a new business venture. Remember, networking goes beyond handing out business cards and attending meet-ups. What you should focus on is building relationships. Here, I am referring to both professional as well as personal relationships. Lack of a trustworthy network cannot save your startup from risks and eventual failure to launch. Additionally, small scale businesses are more vulnerable to failure due to a poor network. This is even more relevant if your business is specific to a location or a region. Without a well established network it is impossible to generate curiosity about your product and expect its successful takeoff.

16. Wrong Timing

To say the least, timing can make or break. Product inception, execution, marketing, and launch are all useless if you are in the right place at the wrong time. Poorly timed ventures are doomed for failure irrespective of how unique and robust their product offering is. The timing is beyond any entrepreneur's control and luck plays a fair role in this.

Take for instance Twitter. If the social platform was launched in 2016 instead of 2006, no one would have given it a second thought. While it would have served the purpose that is fulfilling today, the market would have been too saturated for attracting a user base. Also, in all likelihood, twitter would then have been a late entrant. Looking at the other side of the coin, there are companies like WebTV that had a brilliant product offering, but their timing just wasn't right. The product allowed viewers to surf web on the TV, hence, the name. Even though it brought the internet to the living room, it was 20 years too early. The industry itself was not ready for this kind of product innovation. For example, the content on internet was not designed to be read on TV back then. It was meant entirely for the desktop viewing comfort.

17. Late Entrant

Every business has pioneers as well as followers. While the success level of pioneers is always higher, there is no surety that followers can learn and launch with a better model. However, being a late entrant in any market means that all good ideas are already taken up and you will have to work much harder to make sure that your product stands out and becomes a preferred option. Toyota was certainly not a pioneer but still managed to give competition to the existing well-established brands. On the other hand, a reactive product like Google Hangouts failed to take off as the market was already saturated by similar products which were doing well. It proposed nothing unique that was not being covered by existing products like Skype, Zoom, and Microsoft Teams. As a late entrant, it failed to provide, even the most loyal Google users, a good enough reason to migrate.

18. Discord Among Partners

Harmony in any relationship is essential for its smooth functioning. Just how a marital discord can cause a rift, likewise, a business partnership can go through rough patches every now and then. Startups are more vulnerable to such disputes as everyone is overworked and tensions run high. If partners don't see eye to eye on important matters and have contrasting visions for the startup, it can lead to failure and destruction.

The English rock band, Beetles, left many heartbroken when they announced their breakup. As a group that produced music which has influenced generations, Beatles failed to maintain harmony. In spite of their success, the discords between the members led to the band's untimely demise.

The US based pizza chain, Papa John's is another good example to highlight the impact founders can have on their startups. It founder, John Schnatter, was forced out of the company and has been trying to regain the control as he still holds nearly 30% stake in the organization. This is severely damaging the company's reputation and affecting its bottom line.

19. Fraud

According to Lutz Kauffman, the German economist, startups are more vulnerable to frauds than established business houses. This is because a startup is trying to create its own space in an existing, often crowded market, that can tempt them to bend rules to suit their purpose. The entrepreneurs are also more than likely to be deceived in the early years of their business. You have to be wary of both the partners as well as suppliers as they can take you for a ride knowing that you are new in this area and may lack the required expertise.

Theranos, a blood testing organization had to fold its business after the top executives were accused of massive fraud. The scandal was brought to light in an article in the Wall Street Journal exposing the company's fake claims on their products. It was only upon further investigation that the extent of fraud was revealed which shook the corporate world to its very core.

20. Lack of Innovation

You might have been able to generate interest in your product offering when it was first launched but are unable to retain that leadership position for long. The answer could lie in a lack of innovation on your part. Today's solutions can solve the problems that are here and now. However, change is the only constant and problems are changing every day. If you are unable to innovate and improve the capabilities of your products, the competition is sure to take over and render your product pointless.

While the industry is replete with examples of companies which failed due to lack of innovation, Kodak is one of the biggest such failures till date. As a pioneer that changed the very dynamics of the photography industry, Kodak failed to innovate and stay abreast of the changing times. And, this is one of the major reasons why Kodak was forced to file for Chapter 11 bankruptcy in 2012.

Another interesting example is that of Nokia. The company failed miserably at innovating keeping in line with the market demand. Instead the mobile phone manufacturer focused on selling volumes at low prices to attract the customer and the market was soon overtaken by the likes of Samsung, Blackberry, Apple, Huawei, etc, that were acutely of the direction that the market was heading for.

Looking at the other side of the story, the retail giant Target, has not just managed to innovate but has adapted successfully to the constantly changing client requirements. The effort spent by the business house in establishing and running a design lab has paid off as a third of Target's total revenues are now being generated by their own brand labels.

Innovation is the one thing that will remain constant across all successful business ventures. You can't hope to succeed if you stay rooted in older technology or archaic processes. It is also important to innovate your internal operations along with your product offerings. Brainstorm with your team and find out how you can increase efficiency and deliver better products at a faster speed.

While all of the above mentioned points can spell disaster, avoiding them or doing the exact opposite of what is mentioned above can also potentially turn around your business and expand it to greater heights. The next section highlights these points in reverse and lists out additional measures you can follow to make sure that the startup stays in green.

How To Avoid and Overcome the Failure of Your Startup

Irrespective of the extent to which you have planned the launch of your startup venture, the probability of success to failure remains 50:50. On paper you might have done your calculations and checked all the boxes, but in reality there are forces beyond your direct control that can impact your business. The compilation of 20 reasons discussed above, is not exhaustive and is increasing as new challenges get introduced in the market. So, how does one ensure that the new venture lives and thrives to become a leader in its market space? For starters, avoid getting stuck in any of the 20 potholes mentioned above. Also, the following suggestions are aimed at helping you sail through the tumultuous waters that you are bound to face in the early stages of your business venture.

✓ Failure Can Be Positive

To begin with, it is never a good idea to launch a business on a negative note, so don't start with a fear of failing. On the contrary, some setbacks can actually help your business provided they are small in scale and you learn from them. Failing simply means not obtaining the result you had aimed for. You can analyze what you did wrong and restart the process until you achieve the required result. Apple Inc. is an excellent example of a startup that succeeded and then failed only to start fresh and create a niche for itself where it remains unchallenged today. The company began its operations in the garage of Job's parent's house in California and launched its first product that same year. It was not until 1979 that Jobs shifted the startup's focus to building products with GUI. 1984 and '85 are critical years in Apple's history. Macintosh was launched in 1984 and following Steve Job's exit in 1985. After a series of failed products and misfits, Apple re-assigned the top position to Steve Jobs and the first ever iMac was launched in 1998. Staying in touch with the times, Apple introduces iPod in 2001 and iTunes in 2003. The much revered iPhone was launched 4 years later in 2007 and took the world by storm. There has been no turning back since then. Even with the passing away of it founder, Apple Inc. has managed to retain and improve its position on the leaderboard.

✓ Consistent and Constant

Don't stop, keep going. Giving up on every small hiccup that comes along the road is not the best way to establish a successful business. The key is to be consistent in your effort and to do this constantly. If you are venturing out of your comfort zone, then face your fears head-on and turn them around into acting as positive motivators for your business's success. Had Einstein given up after the first few attempts the world would have remained devoid of all the amazing innovations that are credited to his name. As one of the world's greatest minds, Einstein is today credited with establishing theory that have led to innovations in the future. Most notably, his Theory of Relativity gave an entirely new direction to how we study the science of time, space, gravity, matter, and energy. Today it forms the very basis of study surrounding nuclear energy.

✓ Solutionize!

Don't spend your precious time focusing on the problems at hand. Instead, look for different solutions with which you can try and fix those problems. Once you learn to view every problem as an opportunity to discover solutions, you can truly succeed as an entrepreneur in whichever field you choose to venture into. Work on the complaints that come from your employees, customers, or suppliers. If you can transform them into innovative solutions, that will give you an opportunity to make these bonds stronger than ever.

✓ Begin Small and Scale Up

While the mantra today may seem to be 'go big or go home' but starting at small scale can shield you from putting all your eggs in one basket and avoiding complete disaster. Begin with what you feel you can handle, test the waters, and if you perceive them to be favorable then gradually scale up. Be on a constant look out for opportunities where you can grow and expand without exposing yourself and your business to risky situations. You and your team are more likely to be motivated if you achieve positive results in the early stages of your startup. These achievements can act as encouragements and push you towards broadening your horizons in a more assured manner. A motivated team will definitely be a more efficient one as well. Starting on these little positive notes can turn out to be the best strategy for setting up your new business venture. Shopify is an excellent example of starting small. The venture began as a search for a simple shopping cart solution and was fully blown into a revenue generating business in just 6 years. At the time of its IPO Shopify was valued at 14 billion dollars.

- ✓ **Financial Management**

Financial management is one of the strongest pillars on which you can erect your new enterprise successfully. As a wider term, Financial management can involve everything pertaining to monetary transactions in your startup - working capital, salaries, cashflow, debts, loans, etc. Also, maintaining an effective cash flow can make sure that your business stays afloat with capability to expand in the future. It is also essential to make sure that you are able to pay for all the expenses you incur and meet your financial commitments.

You can also induce effective financial management by making sure that you invoice on time and follow up for collections to ensure that you receive your payments on time. This can also help you manage debt and make sure that you don't lag behind in loan repayments. While a do-it-yourself attitude is always the mantra in a startup, here it will make more sense to hire the services of a financial expert who can advise you as to how best you can optimize the use of available funds. A financial advisor can also make sure that you work within the confines of rules and regulations. It is important to avoid undertaking any undue risks which can harm your business.

- ✓ **Envision**

Have a clear vision when you launch a startup. Be firm in what you want to achieve and the milestones you want to create. This will not just provide a structure to your entire enterprise but will also help you envisage the potential obstacles and you will be better equipped to face them. The vision you have for your business can cover areas such as the mission statement, the niche you want to service, the go-to market strategies, how you intend to handle competition, etc. It is important to remain realistic while setting up or modifying your vision. Be aware of your limitations and find ways to work around them so that you can be successful. The vision you set will ultimately define the outcome you want to achieve. Take Microsoft for example; their vision, when the company was founded, was simple yet effective - 'A computer on every desk and every home.' Even though their vision has undergone changes with the passage of time and changing technology, the company has remained true to its core values. This is a major contributor towards the immense success that the organization has enjoyed in the last few decades.

- ✓ **Analyze**

The key is to constantly analyze, assess, and reassess your internal and external strengths and weaknesses so you are under no illusions regarding your business's situation. Try and have a clear breakdown of your strengths, weaknesses, opportunities, and threats at any given point in time so that you can clearly see where you lack. If you have a clear assessment of your startup's current situation then, you can take appropriate measures to fill any gaps that may be open. Analyze each component separately and then collectively to arrive at the best course of action. If you are able to perform this activity regularly and correctly, there is no way that success will not find a way towards your startup.

✓ Never Say Die!

Startups are hard work and can prove difficult even for the toughest minds. There will be times when you will second guess your decisions. However, doubting your faith and capabilities can prove to be fatal for your fledgling business venture. It is important to understand that every new phase of life comes with a set of challenges that can affect your self-esteem and make you feel unsure as to the best course of action that you should take. At such times, it is imperative that you retain faith in your abilities and find out avenues where you can seek help from. Failure and setbacks are a part of life in general and giving up is never the solution that you should resort to. Had Steve Jobs given up after being thrown out of his own startup the mobile phone market might have missed the revolution that was brought on by Apple's flagship products. It was because Steve Jobs refused to give in to failure (personal and professional) that he was able to turn around his life and create something even more brilliant. The success of his 2nd venture NeXT, effectively, re-opened the gates for his return to Apple as CEO in 1997.

✓ Networking

The situations and challenges mentioned above will definitely test your strength, but you can overcome these if you have an effective personal and professional network in place. In today's social age and time, a well-established network can help you market your product better. Through your circle you can create the required buzz even before your venture is launched.

Networking can be a fun activity that can boost your confidence. It is essential for personal growth as well as new business development. This is probably the cheapest way to promote and grow your business. Networking is something we all do, knowingly or unknowingly, in our daily lives. So, what is stopping you from giving it a direction and marketing your product or abilities through it?

Networking done right can help you stay abreast of competition as well. You can also come across opportunities to meet potential financial investors or partners. A supportive network can come in handy when you are facing problems. If nothing else, your friends can be understanding and supportive at a time when you need it the most. You may be surprised at the extent of opportunities that you can discover when you network in the relevant circles. Whether it is life, business, or politics, Networking will never go out of fashion. It will remain an essential ingredient in the recipe for success.

✓ Think Like The Client

Put yourself in your client's shoes and try to study the issues you are facing from their point of view. For this, you need to establish an effective feedback and communication mechanism. Once that is done, be prepared for negative as well as positive feedback and review it objectively. You can keep your product relevant and keep your clients happy once you learn to accept and accordingly act on the reviews and feedbacks left by them.

✓ Continuous Innovation

Don't stop innovating, because your competitor will not. Even if you have created a niche for your product where you are a pioneer, you need to innovate and rejuvenate your product constantly to keep it relevant and remain at the top position. Basking in the glory of your initial success and ignoring the Research & Development wing can prove to be fatal for your business. This is primarily because competition will always catch up and you can't monopolize an area for long. Few companies like, The Walt Disney, are able to understand and overcome this obstacle. Walt Disney's products are as attractive for children of today as they were when the company was launched decades ago. 30 years ago, they recreated the magical fairy tales from children's favorite story books (The little Mermaid) and brought them to life on screen. Even though the traditional fairy tales have given way to a more modern tale (e.g. Frozen), the appeal and popularity has not diminished.

✓ Leadership

There are numerous examples of startups that had innovative product offerings but failed to take off due to lack of effective leadership. The leadership role is more important in a startup than it is in an organization with years of experience behind it. He or she is not just the generator of the idea but is essentially the one who makes the important decisions, build a strong team and establishes the company's image. Therefore, leadership goes a long way in determining whether the new business venture will succeed or fail. For instance, Beepi, a used car online marketplace failed to make its mark due to ineffective management and lack of leadership. Even though the startup was successful in raising funds, its poor management left them in a lurch. It finally closed down in 2017 with barely half a decade in business.

✓ Solid Foundation

At the core of it, a startup is primarily a business aiming to make profits. Therefore, it should be guided by all the fundamentals that pertain to business principles and practices. Avoid getting too involved in your product that you refuse to acknowledge its flaws. Take Blackberry for example. The Canadian smartphone maker pioneered the business phone model but refused to adapt to the growing android market. It was as late as 2015 when the phone maker released its android-based smartphones. However, by that time it was too late as Blackberry had lost out its market share to the likes of Samsung, Apple, Huawei etc. Therefore, it is important to constantly check the basis of your being in business. Launching products or services that are true to your brand image but not relevant to times will not help your venture succeed. Don't refrain from making tough decisions, if required. Such decisions can turn around the fortunes of your dwindling startup.

✓ Are You Ready?

Lastly, not everyone is cut out to be an entrepreneur. But that's alright. It may just mean that you require more time to hone your entrepreneurial skills before you can leave the confines of employment and start out on your own. Apart from acquiring, launching a startup takes an immense amount of skill and energy, not to mention the risk associated with it. If you don't have an appetite for taking risk, no amount of training can help you acquire this trait. According to recent statistics, nearly 70% of startups close business within their first ten years of operations. Also, only 40% of startups can turn around profits and over 80% of startup ventures face severe cash flow problems. If you are thinking of entering into the domain of entrepreneurs, then you must be willing to accept these (any other) challenges and devise an effective strategy to overcome them. Overall, you must surround yourself with strong, like-minded people who share your vision, and be ready to lead them to the best of your abilities.

Conclusion

The prospect of launching a new business venture comes with an entourage of risks and worries, even though we see a far healthier crop of entrepreneurs than we did a few decades ago. We know that the rate of failure is higher than the rate of success, and the probability that a business might succeed can keep a true entrepreneur motivated. The ones who are successful not only have a vision but are also able to consistently grow and expand their business while offsetting risks and increasing their revenues bit by bit.

Being patient is not akin to laziness. Just because you are not reacting does not mean that you are lazing around. It simply means being on the lookout for appropriate opportunities and then grabbing them with both hands. Successful business owners are able to recognize this important character trait and are able to extract full benefits from advantageous situations. It's okay to wait if you feel the market is not ready for your product or if the timing is not appropriate for an upgrade.

Lastly, never cross your legal and financial boundaries. You can bounce back from failed products and again, Apple Inc. is an excellent example. But you can never re-enter the market if you are caught red-handed in an illegal issue, otherwise you can then say goodbye to your dream of launching a successful startup. Business works on trust and while building it can take a lifetime, the destruction of trust can take but a few seconds. By getting involved in illegal activities, you are exposing your product to litigation as well.

When you are up against severe odds, it is best to remain strong and have faith in your capabilities. Build resilience and learn from the mistakes of others. Have a trustworthy network that you can rely on for support and be prepared to offer similar services to them if and when required. The archives are filled with anecdotes that can educate you through the examples of those that have travelled this treacherous path before you. The key lies in the fact that you have to first, find a way to survive as a startup. Once you have achieved this you can continue to thrive as an industry leader with innovation, skill and technology.

References

- https://hbr.org/2018/10/startups-are-more-vulnerable-to-fraud-heres-why
- https://www.cbinsights.com/research/biggest-startup-failures/
- https://hbr.org/2019/10/5-things-leaders-do-that-stifle-innovation
- https://www.forbes.com/sites/theyec/2019/09/23/fatal-startup-pitfalls-dos-and-donts-to-avoid-them/#372b56074a35
- http://www.theinvestor.co.kr/view.php?ud=20190904000704
- https://www.businessinsider.com.au/signs-not-ready-to-start-your-own-business-2018-11?r=US&IR=T
- https://en.wikipedia.org/wiki/Microsoft
- https://www.businessinsider.com.au/signs-not-ready-to-start-your-own-business-2018-11?r=US&IR=T
- https://www.cnbc.com/2017/07/10/jawbones-demise-a-case-of-death-by-overfunding-in-silicon-valley.html
- https://www.forbes.com/sites/forbestechcouncil/2019/06/14/how-did-wework-beat-regus/#6e8c03604303
- https://www.marketing-interactive.com/carrefour-what-went-wrong-2/
- https://www.entrepreneur.com/article/288769
- https://en.wikipedia.org/wiki/Kodak
- https://en.wikipedia.org/wiki/MSN_TV
- https://www.virgin.com/entrepreneur/richard-branson-the-importance-of-passion-in-business

www.ingramcontent.com/pod-product-compliance
Lightning Source LLC
Chambersburg PA
CBHW031512210526
45463CB00008B/3213